PUSS IN SLIPPERS

A Panto–Minidrama with no boots on

by

RICHARD TYDEMAN

Samuel French – London
New York – Sydney – Toronto – Hollywood

FOR AMATEUR PRODUCTION ENQUIRIES

UNITED KINGDOM AND WORLD
EXCLUDING NORTH AMERICA
plays@samuelfrench.co.uk
020 7255 4302/01

Each title is subject to availability from Samuel French,
depending upon country of performance.

CHARACTERS

in order of their appearance

COMPERE, *who has a book*
LAWYER, *who reads the Miller's will*
PATIENCE
YUM-YUM } *The Miller's daughters,*
LITTLE BUTTERCUP } *beneficiaries of the will*
PUSS, *one of the bequests*
DACIUS, *King of the Land of Marjerene*
QUEEN, *his Mother*
CHAMBERLAIN, *an optional extra*
MARY
GRACE } *Ladies of the Court*
LETITIA
Other Courtiers, and Voice of the Ogre (off)

Scenes: An Ancient Mill
A Royal Palace
The Ogre's Mansion

This Panto-Minidrama follows in the tradition of *Red Hot Cinders, Forty Winks Beauty, Ali's Barbara, Snow White Special, Albert Laddin, Little Red Whittington,* and *Who's Bean Stalking?* It is just as easy to learn, costume and produce.

PRODUCTION NOTE

The Compere is the pivot on which the Minidrama revolves. Having a copy of the script, he can also act as prompter and keep the show going. His costume could be evening dress, a pierrot outfit, or whatever happens to be available. The Compere could also, of course, be a lady.

The rest of the costumes could either be in that delightfully indeterminate fairy story period so popular in pantomime, or else in modern dress. Puss can be in a complete animal costume if preferred; but probably it would be better just to dress her in black sweater and jeans, stitch a couple of ears on a black cap, and paint three large whiskers sticking out on each side of her face. Do not attempt to dress the Miller's three daughters to resemble the Gilbertian characters whose names they bear; the Miller's sense of humour did not quite extend as far as that, and it would only cause confusion.

Scenery should only be used if you can change it in the very brief time that the curtain is down. Otherwise a curtain setting is best, using different chairs for each scene.

The appearance of the mouse in the second scene can best be effected by making the mouse completely imaginary. Make sure that everyone knows exactly the spot on the floor where the mouse is supposed to be, and then let them all stare at that spot until Puss has scooped the mouse up. The Ogre does not appear either, except in the form of various animals, but his voice should be deep and strong, if possible amplified through a loudspeaker in the wings, or through a megaphone. The Chamberlain is put down as an optional extra in the cast list, because his part could be read by the Compere if you are short of actors—though obviously it is better to have a real Chamberlain if you can.

Keep the rhythm of the atrocious verse, and let each player speak only the words written for him—neither more nor less. In this way you will get the maximum fun out of the Minidrama, both for your audience and for yourselves.

R.T.

PUSS IN SLIPPERS

> *The* COMPERE *enters, in front of curtains, carrying a copy of the script.*

COMPERE. Hullo, and here we are again!
  So brace yourselves to take the strain,
  And bid farewell to rhyme and reason,
  For now we're in the panto season.

  Tonight, without the least excuse,
  We very proudly introduce
  To all you mums and dads and nippers,
  Our mini-panto, "Puss In Slippers".

  What's that, my dear? You always thought
  It should be "Boots"? Perhaps it ought
  In ordinary pantomime.
  Not here! Now, once upon a time
  A certain miller went and died.
  So, curtain up. (*Curtain rises.*) Let's look inside,
  And here, within the ancient mill
  The family lawyer reads the will.

> (*The* LAWYER *is sitting, reading will to the miller's three daughters,* PATIENCE, YUM-YUM *and* BUTTERCUP.)

LAWYER. Your late dear father here directs
  That his estate and his effects,
  His property and living quarters,
  Shall all be left to his three daughters;
  Between you they're divided up—
  Patience, Yum-Yum and Buttercup.
COMPERE. He was devoted, that old man,
  To Gilbert and to Sullivan.
LAWYER. Patience, he hopes, will take the mill.
PATIENCE. Oh dear Papa! Of course I will.
LAWYER. To Yum-Yum he has left his ass.
YUM-YUM. A fortune I shall soon amass!
LAWYER. To Buttercup he leaves his cat.
BUTTERCUP. Oh gosh, I don't think much of that!
LAWYER. He adds that Buttercup's bequest
  Could easily turn out the best.
> (*Rising and shaking hands.*)
  And now I'll say good afternoon.
  I have to see an ogre soon—
  A highly influential client
P.S.*

Who's charged with murdering a giant.
With any luck I think they oughter
Bring it in as giant-slaughter.
                    (*He goes out.*)
COMPERE. The sisters now draw in their chairs
   And talk about their own affairs.
PATIENCE. This dear old mill is simply made
   For boosting up the tourist trade.
   We'll advertise it in the town
   With dainty teas at half-a-crown.
YUM-YUM. We'll soon be making quids and quids—
   And tourists always bring their kids;
   We'll serve ice-lollies, and besides,
   The ass can give them donkey-rides.
BUTTERCUP. A cat! I ask you, what the dickens
   Can I do while you count your chickens?
   If only I'd been left a cow.
                    (*Enter* PUSS.)
   Here comes the wretched creature now.
         (PUSS *kneels by* BUTTERCUP, *purring and rubbing head against*
      her.)
YUM-YUM (*rising*). Well, come on Patience, let's begin,
   And soon our fortune we shall win.
PATIENCE (*rising*). We'll get an advert in the *Star*.
   For barbecue and coffee-bar.
YUM-YUM. We'll build a stage.
PATIENCE.   We'll hire a band.
YUM-YUM. How marvellous!
PATIENCE.   How simply grand!
            (PATIENCE *and* YUM-YUM *go out.*)
COMPERE. Now Buttercup is left, and she
   Has only Puss for company.
   To whom she puts a question, thus:
BUTTERCUP. Oh Pussy, what's the use of us?
   I can't afford to buy you kippers.
PUSS. I'd rather have a pair of slippers.
               (BUTTERCUP *jumps up with a cry.*)
COMPERE. No wonder that she gives a squawk
   On hearing that her cat can talk—
   And talk in English, if you please,
   Not Persian, Manx or Siamese.
PUSS. I am no ordinary cat.
COMPERE. Quite so. We had suspected that.
PUSS. Give me a pair of slippers, and
   I'll make you Queen of all this land.
            (COMPERE *hands* BUTTERCUP *a pair of slippers.*)

BUTTERCUP. The only slippers I possess
  Are these. But will they fit you?
PUSS (*putting them on*).   Yes.
  Your fortune's made. Just follow me,
  And you shall see what you shall see.
           (PUSS *departs followed by* BUTTERCUP.)
COMPERE. What's that? You still think "boots" is better?
  Don't speak too loud: you might upset her.
  This puss is quite a fashion-plate,
  And boots are hardly up-to-date.
      (*Re-enter* PATIENCE *and* YUM-YUM *with some books of music.*)
PATIENCE. Oh Buttercup, we want you, dear,—
  How very odd; she isn't here.
COMPERE. She's just gone out to feed the cat.
  But tell us, what are you two at?
YUM-YUM. We want some capital; so we
  Are selling father's libraree.
PATIENCE. We ought to raise a good commission
  On "Iolanthe", first edition.
YUM-YUM. We hope to get, by trying hard,
  A pound for "Yeomen of the Guard".
PATIENCE. This "Sorcerer" is not too clean.
YUM-YUM. You think, ten bob?
PATIENCE.   We'll try fifteen.
YUM-YUM. What shall we do with "Princess Ida"?
PATIENCE. Give her away. I can't abide her.
YUM-YUM. We'll sell four operas for a start.
             (*They begin to move away.*) ·
COMPERE. Oh shades of Richard D'Oyley Carte!
  Curtain! (*Curtain falls, leaving* COMPERE *outside.*)
      Savoy, now toll your bells,
  And tell it not in Sadlers Wells,
         (*With exaggerated tragic gestures.*)
  O Golders Green, go shed your tears
  For "Pirates" and for "Gondoliers".
  With such impertinent bravado,
  These girls would even sell "Mikado"!
      (*In a complete change of voice back to normal.*)
  At this point usually I pause
  To give you time for your applause.
         (*Starts to clap himself.*)
  I really think I'm pretty good,
  Don't you? (*Someone at back of audience claps twice.*) I thought you
    would.
      (*Someone at back of audience makes a rude noise.*)
  Enough of that, or you will sure

Be apex over Pinafore!
      (LAWYER *appears in front of curtain clasping a book of music.*)
LAWYER. Oh dear, I don't know what to do.
COMPERE. I thought we'd seen the last of you.
LAWYER. Yes, so did I. My client in fury
  Insisted on a Trial by Jury.
  He frightened all the jury so—
COMPERE. They let him off?
LAWYER.   Oh dear me, no,
  They said he must be hanged today—
  And that was when he broke away.
COMPERE. You mean that dreadful ogre's free?
LAWYER. Indeed. I fear he's after me.
  Please help me. Take this precious score,
         (*Hands* COMPERE *the music book.*)
  I've got to save my "Ruddigore".
             (*He runs off.*)
COMPERE. I can't think of another title,
  So that concludes tonight's recital.
  Now we must take our story up
  With slippered puss and Buttercup.
  That clever cat, as you have seen,
  Has sworn to make its mistress queen;—
  In such a case the easiest thing
  Would be to wed her to a king.
  So, Curtain up! (*Curtain rises.*) Ah, what a sight,—
     (*Young* KING DACIUS *sits on throne. His mother the* QUEEN
  stands on his R., *with the* CHAMBERLAIN *next to her.* COURTIERS
  grouped round.)
  Such regal splendour dazzling bright!
  For on his throne here can be seen
  King Dacius of Marjerene.
DACIUS. Good morning friends. I'm glad you've come.
QUEEN. Be quiet, Dacey.
DACIUS.   Sorry, Mum.
COMPERE. As you'll observe, the youthful king's
  Still tied to Mother's apron-strings.
QUEEN. My son, you've reached the time of life
  When young men like to choose a wife.
DACIUS. To choose! Oh Mum, you mean I'm free—
QUEEN. The choosing will be done by me.
       (*To* MARY, *one of the Court ladies.*)
  Come forward you. Your name and rank?
MARY. The Honorable Mary Blank.
CHAMBERLAIN (*reading from a large book, to* QUEEN). Top deb of
  teen fifty-eight.

Father a minister of state.
Small town house and county manor.
Thousand a year. Plays the pianner.
QUEEN. Next.
GRACE.　　　　　The Lady Grace Carew.
CHAMBERLAIN. Roedean and Girton. Hockey blue.
　Father from Canada; travelled steerage,
　Invented fish-cakes; given a peerage.
QUEEN. Number three.
LETITIA.　　　　　　　　Letitia Gunning.
CHAMBERLAIN. Miss Tooting Bec, three seasons running.
　Parents unknown, but statistics—
　Forty, twenty, thirty-six.
DACIUS. Coo Mum!
QUEEN.　　　　　　Be quiet. Number four.
CHAMBERLAIN. I fear we haven't any more.
QUEEN. No more? But what about these others?
CHAMBERLAIN. They've all been sent here by their mothers.
QUEEN. Quite so. That means they're either dim,
　Or much too weak to manage (*Indicating* DACIUS.) him.
COMPERE. Now while the Queen and all the Court
　Are sunk in contemplative thought,
　A cry goes up throughout the house—
HALF THE COURTIERS. Oh help!
THE OTHER HALF.　　　　　Oh help!
ALL.　　　　　　　　　　　A mouse! A mouse!
　　　(DACIUS *stands on throne.* QUEEN *raises her skirts. Courtiers
　cling to each other in terror, all staring at "mouse". See Production
　Note.*)
COMPERE. This is a type of mass paralysis
　Which quite defies all sane analysis,—
　That grown-up people lose their heads
　Before such tiny quadrupeds.
　Again they cry:—
ALL.　　　　　　A cat! A cat!
COMPERE. And through the door, in slippers flat,
　　　　　　　　(*Enter* PUSS.)
　Appears our enterprising feline,
　Making towards that mouse a bee-line.
　　　　(PUSS *scoops up mouse and goes out. All recover.*)
　They breathe a sigh of pure relief.
A COURTIER. Such speed is quite beyond belief.
ANOTHER. It's wonderful. And I've heard tell
　This slippered cat can talk as well.
　　　(*Re-enter* PUSS, *dusting her paws together. Bows to* QUEEN *and*
　DACIUS.)

DACIUS. A talking cat? In that case, bless us,
  We'll ask you, Pussy, to address us.
PUSS. Regrets, this morning, I report:
  My mistress could not come to Court.
QUEEN. Her name?
PUSS.   She is referred to as
  The Marchioness of Carrabas.
DACIUS. A Marchioness! And is she pretty?
PUSS. Well-favoured, wealthy, wise and witty.
DACIUS. She sounds the very girl for—
QUEEN (interrupting).   Son,
  It doesn't do to jump the gun.
  Go back most noble cat, and say
  We'll come to tea with her today.
COMPERE. Did you observe how Puss turned white
  On hearing this? And well she might,
  For Buttercup's (excuse my scansion)
  A marchioness without a mansion.
                (PUSS bows and goes.)
QUEEN. The court is over. Minstrels in;
  Let dancing practice now begin.
        (The Court prepares to dance. If desired, a minuet or gavotte
  could now be performed—or of course a Twist. Curtain falls, leaving
  COMPERE outside.)
COMPERE. Now Puss has taken on a task.
  How will she do it? You may ask.
  The only mansion I can see
  Is that old ogre's property;
  And ogres, as I know full well,
  Are never over-keen to sell.
        (PATIENCE and YUM-YUM run on in front of curtain.)
PATIENCE. Oh save us! We have been pursued
  By monstrous ogre, rough and rude.
YUM-YUM. He shouted, brandishing a club,
  "I want my dinner. There's some grub!"
COMPERE. Well, now we're in a pretty mess.
  Are we afraid of ogres?
PATIENCE AND YUM-YUM. Yes!
        (They start to run away. BUTTERCUP and PUSS enter, meeting them.)
BUTTERCUP. Pray have no fear. You shall not die.
  Just leave it all to Puss and I.
COMPERE (to audience). Grammatically, you'll agree,
  She should have said, "to Puss and me".
  But she's a girl of humble station
  Who hasn't had your education.
YUM-YUM. Look out! He's here!

OGRE (*off*).   Ho ho! I see
  My dinner's waiting there for me.
COMPERE. Now Pussy, if you're really clever,
  This is your biggest moment ever.
PUSS (*bowing towards* OGRE'S *voice*). Good day to you, most mighty
  wizard.
OGRE (*off*). Why, bless my liver, heart and gizzard,
  A cat!
PUSS.   Oh sir, we hear that you
  Can do impersonations, too.
OGRE (*off*). I take the shape, just as I wish,
  Of any kind of beast or fish.
                    (PUSS *whispers to* COMPERE.)
COMPERE. What, any kind?
OGRE.   Just name a creature;
  I'll demonstrate before I eat yer.
COMPERE. Supposing then, just for a try on,
  You turn yourself into a lion.
          (*A cardboard cut-out of a lion—or an actor dressed as a lion
  appears from wings.* OGRE'S *voice is heard roaring. Players cling to-
  gether in terror.*)
  That's very wonderful of course.
  And now, suppose you try a horse.
          (*Lion disappears. A horse takes its place.* OGRE'S *voice is heard
  neighing, accompanied by coconut shells.*)
  Big beasts are easy, but the small
  Would be much harder.
OGRE (*off, as horse disappears*). Not at all.
COMPERE. I'm sure that you'd be much too big
  To turn yourself into a pig.
          (*A pig appears,* OGRE *heard grunting and squealing. Pig disap-
  pears.*)
  Well done. You can't get less than that.
OGRE (*off*). Oh can't I! Watch. I'll be—a rat.
          (*A rat appears from wings.* PUSS *pounces on it and goes out.* OGRE'S
  *voice heard bellowing, getting quieter and quieter until all is still.
  Re-enter* PUSS, *dusting her paws together.*)
PUSS. The world has now one ogre less.
  Your mansion waits you, marchioness.
          (*Takes* BUTTERCUP *by the arm, and they go out.*)
COMPERE. Her mansion! Well, I never did
  See such a smooth take-over bid!
  But now we'd better go there, too,
  And see just what they're going to do;
  For they have royal guests for tea,
                (*To* PATIENCE *and* YUM-YUM.)

Come on now, girls, you follow me—
No no, on second thoughts, stand still.
We'll take a short cut. (*Calling.*) Curtains, Bill.
   (*Curtain rises on Ogre's mansion. No one on stage. Two chairs.*
  PATIENCE *and* YUM-YUM *walk about and inspect.*)
PATIENCE. That ogre must have been well-placed.
YUM-YUM. I can't say I admire his taste.
COMPERE. I think it might be rather kind
 To get things ready. Would you mind?
 The guests can not be very far;
 Perhaps you girls would brew the char.
   (PATIENCE *and* YUM-YUM *go. Trumpets sound. Enter from the*
  other side PUSS, *walking backwards and bowing, followed by* QUEEN
  DACIUS *and the Court.*)
PUSS. My gracious mistress bids me greet you;
 And shortly she'll be here to meet you.
   (QUEEN *and* DACIUS *sit. Courtiers group round.*)
QUEEN. We're very pleased to be invited. (PUSS *goes out.*)
DACIUS. Ooh Mum, I'm getting all excited!
QUEEN. Dacey, control yourself at once;
 She'll think that you're a frightful dunce.
   (*Trumpets sound. Enter* PUSS, *walking backwards and bowing.*)
COMPERE (*announcing*). Her Grace the noble Marchioness of Carrabas,
 O.H.M.S.
   (*Enter* BUTTERCUP, *gorgeously dressed.*)
QUEEN (*rising*). Ah, Marchioness, how pleased I am—
BUTTERCUP. My friends all call me "Butter", ma'am.
QUEEN. Then I shall call you Butter, too.
   (*Nudging* DACIUS *who is staring open-mouthed.*)
 Now Dacius, say how-d'ye-do.
DACIUS. Hullo. (*He rises, still gazing.*)
COMPERE.   Poor Dacey's overcome;
 Such loveliness has struck him dumb.
 Yes, this is certainly the Queen
 For Dacey, and for Marjerene.
 But now the lad can only splutter;
 He can't tell Marjerene from Butter.
DACIUS. Will you—?
BUTTERCUP.   Oh yes. (*They clasp hands.*)
COMPERE. Well, that has been
 The fastest thing I've ever seen.
 Puss, hitch your wagon to a star—
 Go, fetch a Marriage Registrar.
   (*Enter* LAWYER.)
LAWYER. Did someone call me?
COMPERE.   Just the man.

Can you take weddings?
LAWYER (*moving between* DACIUS *and* BUTTERCUP). Yes, I can.
COMPERE. Your other client won't be missed;
    He's on the missing ogres list.
    So please proceed without delay.
QUEEN. I'm here to give the groom away.
LAWYER. Quite so. Then, under rule sixteen,
            (*Joining the hands of* DACIUS *and* BUTTERCUP.)
    I now pronounce you King and Queen.
                (*Enter* PATIENCE *and* YUM-YUM *with tea.*)
COMPERE. How splendid. Puss, you've earned your tea.
PUSS (*dusting her paws together after another good job done*). Oh thank you,
    only milk for me.
            (DACIUS *and* BUTTERCUP *sit on chairs.* PUSS *sits on floor at their*
    feet. QUEEN *and* LAWYER *behind chairs.* PATIENCE *and* YUM-YUM
    on either side, with tea. Courtiers suitably grouped. Tableau.)
COMPERE. And thus our mini-panto ends.
    We hope we've pleased you, gentle friends.
    We've lost an ogre, gained a bride,
    And done a good bit more beside.
    While in the land of Marjerene,
    They're happy as a king—and queen.
    The future—you can see their faces,
    Will all be Buttercup's and Dacey's.

    So now we hope we've proved to you
    That whether in a boot or shoe,
    Or mocassins or frogman's flippers,
    There's nothing like a puss in slippers!

                        CURTAIN

9 780573 166129